JEAN CRAIGHEAD GEORGE
LOOK to the NORTH
A Wolf Pup Diary

illustrated by Lucia Washburn

SCHOLASTIC INC.
New York Toronto London Auckland Sydney
Mexico City New Delhi Hong Kong

To Sam
—J.C.G.

To David and my parents
—L.W.

*The illustrations in this book were done in acrylic
on 150-pound Arches watercolor paper.*

Typography by Elynn Cohen

ISBN 0-590-68908-8

12 11 10 9 8 7 6   9/9 0 1 2 3/0

Printed in the U.S.A.   08

First Scholastic printing, November 1998

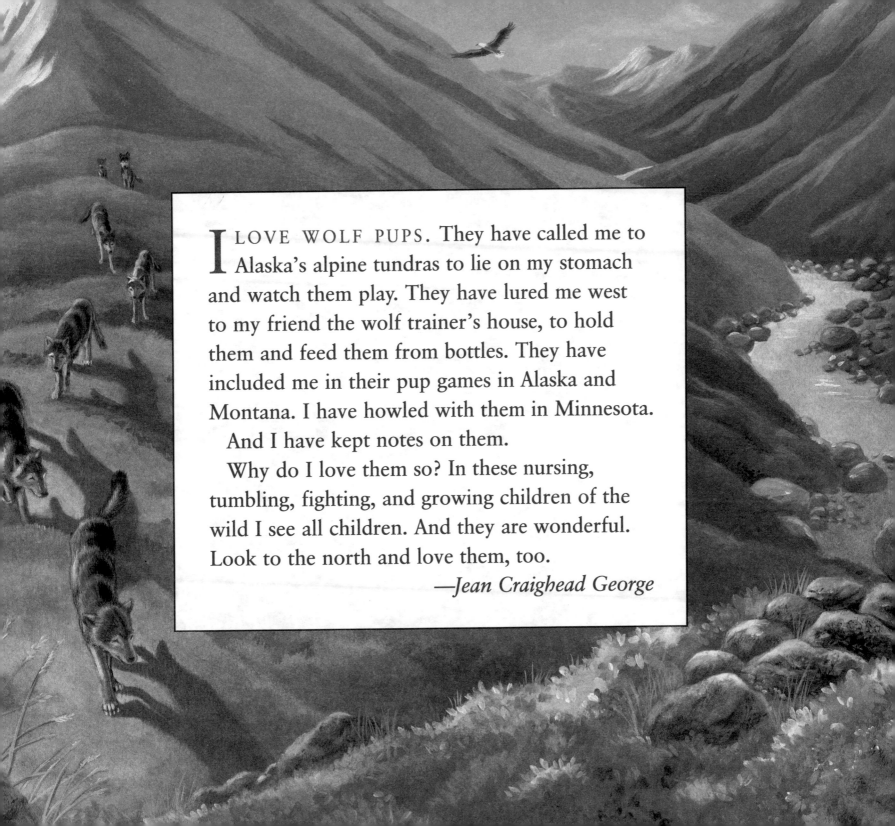

I LOVE WOLF PUPS. They have called me to Alaska's alpine tundras to lie on my stomach and watch them play. They have lured me west to my friend the wolf trainer's house, to hold them and feed them from bottles. They have included me in their pup games in Alaska and Montana. I have howled with them in Minnesota.

And I have kept notes on them.

Why do I love them so? In these nursing, tumbling, fighting, and growing children of the wild I see all children. And they are wonderful. Look to the north and love them, too.

—*Jean Craighead George*

1 Day Old

When you see dandelions turning silver, look to the north. Wolf pups are being born.

Boulder, Scree, and Talus arrive. They are blind and deaf. They can't even smell. Each weighs only one pound. They are curled against their warm mother in a nursery dug deep into a hillside.

Their father is standing in the snow by the den entrance.

The wind blows ice crystals across the cold mountaintop.

10 Days Old

When the yellow warblers return from the south, look to the north. The eyes of the wolf pups are opening.

Boulder sees his sister, Scree, and jumps on her. She knocks him off. He jumps on her again. She bites him with her sharp new baby teeth. He bites her back. They growl their first growls.

Talus nurses. He is the smallest pup.

2 Weeks Old

When the redwings are flashing their bright shoulder badges, look to the north. The mother wolf will take brief vacations.

The mother wolf has not left the pups since they were born. The father fed her while she kept the pups warm. Now the pups are well furred. The mother gets to her feet. The pups are sleeping. She goes down the long tunnel into the sunlight.

She runs joyfully across the alpine tundra, then back to her pack. They run with her.

The pack is small—there are the mother and father, the alphas or leaders; an assistant, the beta; and a yearling male. They run close together like a flock of wheeling birds, never touching. Their ruffs ripple.

3 Weeks Old

When the spring azure blue butterflies are flitting, look to the north. The wolf pups can hear.

Boulder hears his pack howl. He stands up and listens. Scree hears the lambs of the mountain sheep bleating. Talus not only can hear all this, but can also smell it. Talus has a talent. He wobbles out of the den following the sweet scent of morning. Boulder and Scree follow him into the daylight.

The outdoors is bright and big. Boulder jumps on Scree and growls. She turns and bites his neck. He yelps. Talus follows the scent of a lemming and runs smack into his mother. With a low growl she turns him back and stops Scree from shaking Boulder by the neck. The pups scurry into the den.

4 Weeks Old

When you see baby robins, look to the north. Wolf pups are almost weaned.

The mother leaves the pups. The yearling is baby-sitter.

Boulder grabs Scree by the back of her neck and shakes hard. She yelps piteously, then grabs Boulder's neck. He breaks loose. Suddenly Scree rolls to her back, flashing her pale belly fur. This is the wolves' white flag of surrender. Boulder has won. He is alpha pup.

Scree, who is now his assistant, jumps on Talus and growls. Talus smells defeat and flashes his white flag. Scree stops biting.

Each pup has found his or her place in the pup society. They know who they are. All fighting ceases.

7 Weeks Old

*On the longest day of the year, look to the
north. Wolf pups are outdoors playing.*

Boulder, Scree, and Talus are jumping
on the baby-sitter. They chew his tail.
They knock his feet out from under him.
They play rough.

The wolf pack is returning, and Talus
smells the scent of good food on their
breaths.

He sticks his nose in the corner of his
father's mouth, which says in wolf talk,
"I'm a puppy—feed me." The father coughs
up food for Talus. The wolves have brought
food home for the pups in their belly
baskets. The mother stops all milk snacks.

9 Weeks Old

When firecrackers shoot skyward, look to the north. Wolf pups are learning wolf talk.

Boulder, Scree, and Talus can lower their ears to say to their father and mother, "You are the beloved leaders of our pack." They can spank the ground with their front paws to say, "Come play with me," and they can scent mark bones and pretty stones to say, "This is mine."

The wolf den is swathed in blue harebell flowers. The wolves stop and look at them.

10 Weeks Old

When you are eating July's abundant corn on the cob, look to the north. A change is coming to wolfdom.

Talus smells excitement in his mother's sweet scent as she prances before the den. Boulder and Scree cock their heads. The mother suddenly dashes up the den mound and away. The adults trot after her. The pups follow. Not one adult wolf steps on a harebell.

∽

The wolf family arrives at their summer den on a hill above a river. The den is a mere tunnel in which the pups can hide from the eagle, the grizzly bear, and the intense alpine-tundra sun.

The pups play king of the hill, tug-of-war, and football. When they are bored with these games, they play "jump on the baby-sitter."

They dig holes and chew bones, rocks, and puppy tails. Sometimes they chase mice and butterflies.

12 Weeks Old

When the crickets are chirping, look to the north. Wolf pups are learning adult wolf talk.

Boulder can raise his ears straight up to say, "I am the boss pup." He can take Talus's nose gently in his mouth to say, "I'm a good leader." Talus can scent mark to say, "I am irritable." Scree can howl to say, "I am lonely." All three can show their teeth to say, "Hey, watch it." And all three can smile both with their mouths and with their tails.

3 Months Old

When you see the early goldenrod blooming, look to the north. Wolf pups are bonding.

Scree and Talus follow Boulder around berries and over wildflower seeds. They run in a knot, never bumping. They leap as one. They chase birds in a posse. They move across the ridge—until Talus smells a distant grizzly and yips. Then they break ranks and speed home.

16 Weeks Old

When you are eating fresh blueberries, look to the north. Wolf pups are practicing their hunting skills.

Boulder nips Scree the way his father nips caribou. Scree trips Talus the way her mother trips moose. Talus shakes a piece of caribou fur so hard, he gets dizzy. All three can peel hide from the bone toys their parents bring them.

This day the beta does not come home.

The wolves are having trouble getting food without their assistant. It takes the cooperation of many to fell the big game needed to feed a wolf pack. The adults hunt night and day.

4 ½ Months Old

When you are back in school, look to the north. Wolf pups are leaving their summer dens.

Boulder, Scree, and Talus follow their father and mother and the baby-sitter into the valley. They are gypsies. They sleep on open ridges by day and wander the river bottomlands to hunt at night.

Snow is falling in the mountains.

6 Months Old

When you are out trick-or-treating, look to the north. Wolf pups are enrolled in the wolf kindergarten of hunting.

Boulder, Scree, and Talus watch the adults stalk game. They stalk a bird, moving forward in a crouch. They pounce and miss.

Talus hunts by sniffing the air. He picks up the scent of an injured animal and jogs a mile before he finds it. He howls for his pack. They join him and feast.

Talus is no longer the wolf on the bottom. His incredible nose moves him up into a place of high rank. The baby-sitter is now on the bottom.

7 Months Old

When you are eating turkey and watching football, look to the north. The wolf pups are full grown.

Talus smells another wounded animal. The pack follows him through snow and wind drift. They come to a twisted spruce tree. Beneath it lies the beta. He is injured and weak from eating only voles and birds.

The adults fell a caribou. The father brings food to his friend, then scratches a shallow saucer in the snow beside him. He curls up and goes to sleep. The rest of the pack make wolf beds, too. They will take care of the beta until he is well.

10 ½ Months Old

When the day and night are of equal length, look to the north. New pups are on their way.

High up in the mountains, the young adult wolves are ready to help the pack raise their new brothers and sisters.